Right@Sight

a progressive sight-reading course

Violin Grade 5

Caroline Lumsden

ALLE RECHTE VORBEHALTEN · ALL RIGHTS RESERVED

EDITION PETERS
LEIPZIG · LONDON · NEW YORK

Preface

Sight-reading is one of the most important yet neglected aspects of learning an instrument. If treated as an integral and enjoyable part of teaching from an early stage, it is easy to achieve considerable success. The *Right@Sight* series for violin and cello, developed by Caroline Lumsden and Anita Hewitt-Jones, is a very thorough approach that, if followed systematically, will produce excellent sight-readers and will more than prepare students for their graded examinations.

Right@Sight Violin Grade 5 is divided into 2 sections: section 1 (grade 5 – easier) and section 2 (grade 5 – harder). These sections are designed to help students progress smoothly from one grade to the next. A student completing both sections 1 and 2 before taking a grade 5 examination will be supremely confident at sight-reading.

Throughout this book, each double-page spread has a page of solo examples with helpful hints, followed by a page of duets to play with a teacher or friend. Students are encouraged always to use the mnemonic **TRaK** before sight-reading any piece:

> **T**ime signature: always check the time signature of a piece
> **R**hythm: clap the rhythm while saying the time names or singing the note names
> **a**nd
> **K**ey: always check the key signature of a piece and check what finger pattern is needed for that key

There are also *On your own* sections, containing pieces similar to those presented in the exam room – i.e. without any tips.

Encourage pupils to sing with note names – e.g. D E Fs (pronounced "efs"). All sharps have an "s" sound after the note and all flats an "f" sound (e.g. Bf is pronounced "beef"). Good intonation then becomes second nature.

To encourage rhythmic playing, particularly with young children, saying the rhythm in words can help to achieve real success:

Time names	Symbols	Time names	Symbols
slow	♩	trip-le-ty	♩♩♩ (3)
ssh!	𝄽	sh!	𝄾
quick quick	♫	snap-py	♪ ♩.
semiquaver	♬♬	snap-py and	♬♩
quick-semi	♩♬	compound time names	
semi-quick	♬♩	slow	♩.
slow-ow	𝅗𝅥	slow-ow	♩.
slow-ow-ow	𝅗𝅥.	quick-e-ty	♫♩
slow-ow-ow-ow	𝅝	quick-er and	♩.♫
slow-er and	𝅗𝅥. ♪		
quick-er	♩. ♩		

Contents

Section 1 (grade 5 – easier)........................pieces 1–32...................pages 4–21

Section 2 (grade 5 – harder).......................pieces 33–58............pages 22–36

Acknowledgements

Thanks go to Matthew and Charlie Denton, Kate Allott and Kaat Van Bouwel, for suggestions and ideas; also to pupils of Trinity String Time and the Gloucestershire Academy of Music for road testing the material.

© Copyright 2018 by Peters Edition Ltd, London
Cover design by Adam Hay
Music setting by Robin Hagues
Printed in England by Halstan & Co., Amersham, Bucks.

G major, three octaves

Solos

Follow the **TRaK**

1
- **T** Check the time signature and work out the best speed that you can safely play the semiquavers.
- **R** Tap the notes in rhythm on the fingerboard without the bow.
- **K** What is the key? Watch out for any accidentals.
- **?** Where do you shift to 3rd position?

Keep this very lively, using a very short bow for the staccato semiquavers.

2
- **T** What is the time signature?
- **R** Clap the rhythm carefully, noting which bars have *semi-quick* and which *quick-semi*.
- **K** Play the 3 octave scale of G major before you try the piece.
- **?** Where will you shift into 2nd, 3rd and 6th positon and what finger patterns will you use?

*Play very rhythmically with energy in the bow arm and not too fast even though it is **Vivace**.*

! Try to lighten the staccato notes and always look ahead.

Duets

Follow the **TRaK**

3 Don't be caught out by the time signature. Look ahead to the shifting in bars 6–9 before you start. What does *meno mosso* mean?

E minor, two octaves and 4th position

Solos

Follow the **TRaK**

4
- **T** What is the time signature?
- **R** Clap the rhythm carefully. Where is there a tie?
- **K** Which bars tell you that the key is E minor?

Play this through in a lively and rhythmical manner. Watch for the accents.

! Where do you change position and what position do you shift to?

5
- **T** What beat of the bar does this start on?
- **R** Clap the rhythm carefully, giving the minims and the rests their correct value.
- **K** Which bars have accidentals?

Make this lyrical, with a real contrast between phrases.

! Watch for the shift from 3rd to 4th position.

Duets

Follow the **TRaK**

6 *Clap both parts very carefully. Watch for the ties, accents and sudden changes of dynamics.*

G minor, three octaves

Solos

Follow the **TRaK**

7
- **T** What is the value of each beat? How else could the time signature be written?
- **R** Name the notes as you clap in rhythm. i.e. G, D, Eef, A, etc.
- **K** What are the two flats in the key signature?
- **?** What do *risoluto* and **rall.** mean?

Play this with purpose. Look ahead at the accidentals and the shifts.

! Play the scales of both G harmonic and G melodic minors.

8
- **T** What is the time signature? Note where the groups of 5 are 3+2 or 2+3.
- **R** Tap the rhythm through, counting as you go.
- **K** Look at all the bars with accidentals and work out fingerings.
- **!** Watch out for string crossings and practise the shift to 2nd position in the penultimate bar.

Play with a steady five beats per bar and try to observe all the dynamic contrasts.

? What does **Doloroso** and *cresc. molto* mean?

Duets

Follow the **TRaK**

9 *Play this expressively and in time, always listening to the 2nd part.*

Moderato e tranquillo

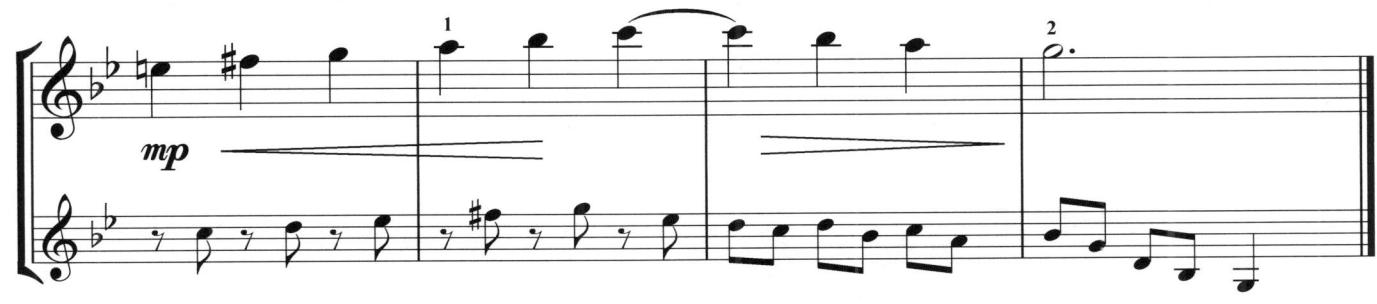

F major, 2nd position

Solos
Follow the **TRaK**

10
- **T** What other time signature can a March be written in?
- **R** Tap the notes in rhythm as you try out the fingerings.
- **K** Play the scale of F major in 2nd position before starting.

Use your bow well for the accents and look ahead to the shifts as you play through firmly.

! Spot the accidental and check the fingerings in bars 10 and 11 before you play!

11
- **T** What does the time signature tell you?
- **R** Keep the rhythm steady, particularly where there are slurs over the bar line.
- **K** What is the key? Beware of unexpected accidentals!
- **!** Try playing this in both 1st position and 2nd position starting on 4th finger. Which is easier?

*Play fairly fast and lift the staccato notes to help create a sense of fun! Watch out for the **rit.** in bar 8.*

Duets

Follow the **TRaK**

12 *Keep this steady yet dance-like. Perhaps try pretend bowing first to decide which beats need a full bow and which a short one.*

Check where the shifts come, and which sections can be played in 2nd position.

Solos

B minor, two octaves

Follow the **TRaK**

13
- **T** What is the time signature?
- **R** Take care with the triplets. How many bars have quavers and triplets?
- **K** What major key shares the same key signature as B minor?

Play firmly and rhythmically in the middle of the bow.

! Look out for accidentals and which bars have a change of position.

14
- **T** What is the time signature and where does it change to compound duple?
- **R** Tap the rhythm of the first four bars, remembering to hold the crotchets for two quaver beats.
- **K** Which bar uses the melodic minor?

Look at the groupings of quavers and semi-quavers before playing through expressively.

! Check the fingering of the 3rd position in bars 6 and 10!

Duets

Follow the **TRaK**

15 *What does mesto mean? Start this in 3rd position. Where do you shift down? Where is there a chromatic passage?*

Play with feeling and a good vibrato!

13

Solos

E major, two octaves

Follow the **TRaK**

16
- **T** What is the time signature?
- **R** Clap very rhythmically with note names, i.e. BB E B Gs etc.
- **K** Which bars use notes of the E major arpeggio?
- **?** Where do you change position and where is there a triplet?

Keep the dotted rhythm and syncopation rhythmical as you play.

17
- **T** What beat of the bar does this start on?
- **R** Clap the rhythm carefully, especially bars 10 and 12.
- **K** Name the sharps in the key signature.
- **?** What does *dolce* mean?

Make this lyrical, with a real contrast between sections.   **!** Watch out for position changes.

Duets

Follow the TRaK

18 *This piece is easy to play if you remember to keep your left hand in 3rd finger pattern with a stretched 3rd finger. What do you notice about both parts at the beginning and the end of bars 8 and 10? What does* **poco rit.** *mean?*

Don't be caught out by the syncopation in bars 13 and 14.

Solos

B major, two octaves

Follow the **TRaK**

19
- **T** What is the time signature? How fast should you play this?
- **R** Tap the notes through in rhythm on the fingerboard (without the bow).
- **K** Play the scale of B major. What finger pattern should you use? Name the sharps in the key signature.

Lift the fingers and tap neatly as you play.

? What does *dim. e rit.* mean?

20
- **T** What is the time signature? Watch for slurs across beats.
- **R** Tap through, working out the fingering, especially the extended 4th finger.
- **K** How many sharps does B major have?

Play this expressively and as smoothly as possible.

? How many 4th finger A♯s are there?

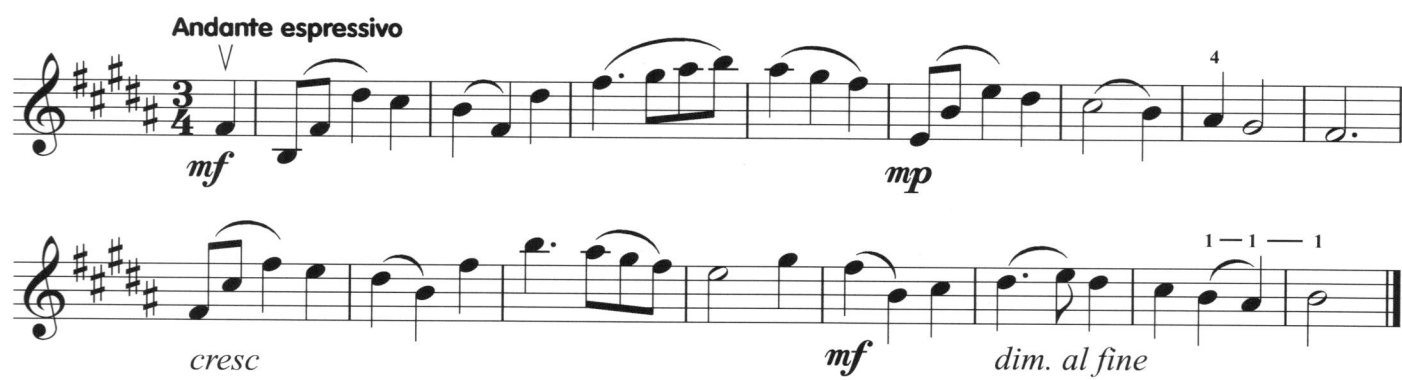

Duets

Follow the TRaK

21 *This piece uses a mixture of 3rd and 4th finger patterns so watch where to stretch that 4th finger! Watch for and prepare the E♯s. Listen carefully to the second part in order to keep this rhythmical and in tune.*

On your own

Solos

Follow the **TRaK**

Remember to check the TRaK as you play through the following examples on your own.

T Look at the time signature. When you have decided how fast to play, keep a steady beat.

R Clap the rhythm, then try any tricky bits on their own. Count carefully and don't try to play too fast.

K The key signature tells you which sharps and flats to play. Think of the fingering you will use. Look to see if there are any scale or arpeggio patterns.

After giving yourself a minute or two to look at all these things, including the expression marks, play through the piece without stopping. Don't panic! Keep going, whatever happens, and play confidently.

22

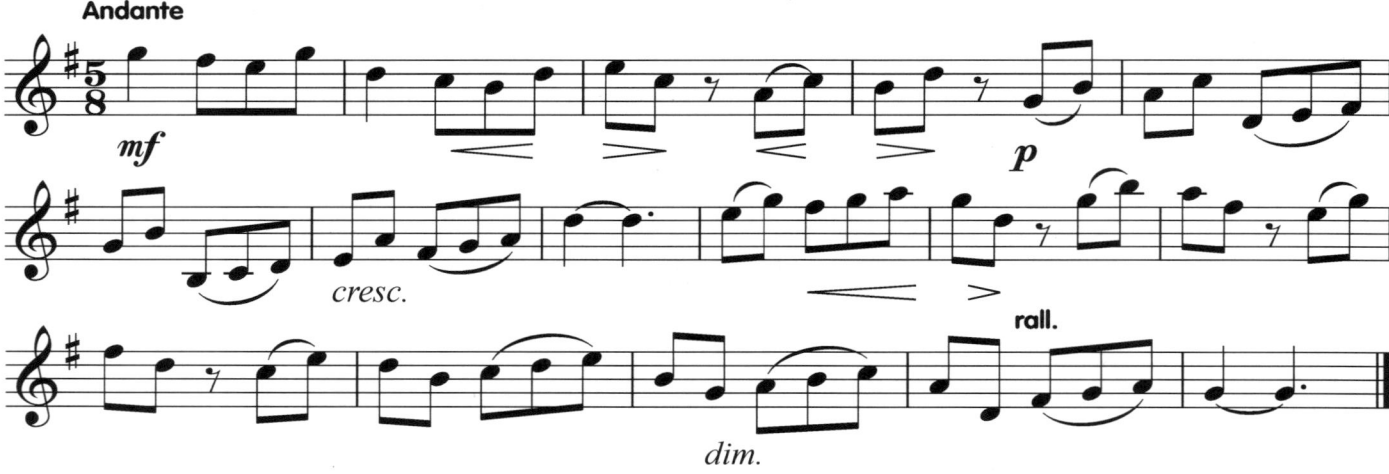

23

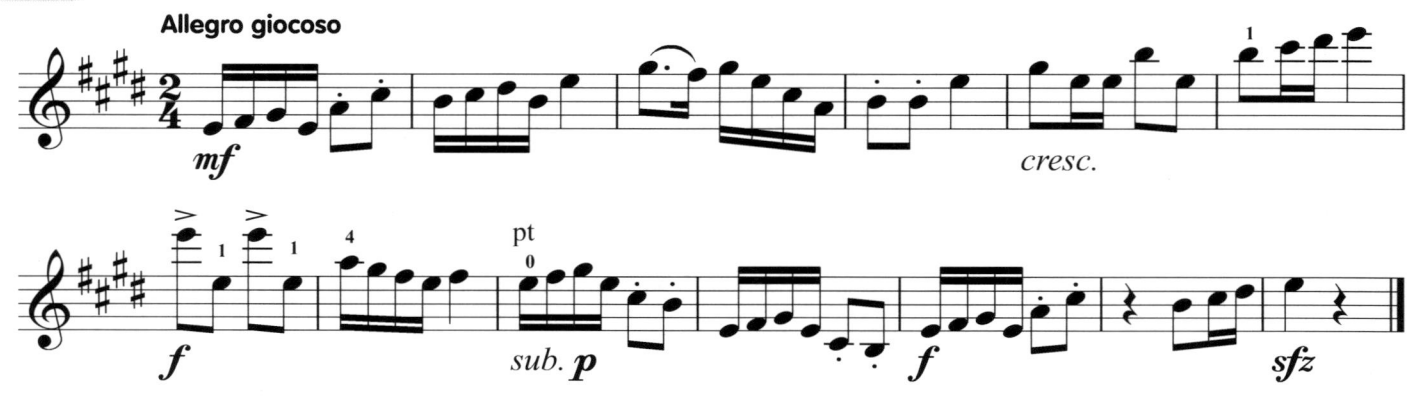

30

31

32

Solos

E♭ major, two octaves

Follow the **TRaK**

33
- **T** How many beats are there in the bar? Which bars have ties?
- **R** Clap the rhythm of bars 3 and 7 before you play.
- **K** Name the flats in the key signature.
- **!** Where do you shift to 4th position? What does **poco rall.** mean? Once you are in 4th position, stay there until the penultimate bar!

Make a real difference between mf and mp as you play.

34
- **T** What is the time signature?
- **R** Clap the rhythm carefully with note names. i.e. B eef G F etc.
- **K** What is the key? Tap the fingering through.

Use whole bows and let this sing.

? Where do you shift to 4th and 3rd position?

Duets

Follow the TRaK

35 *What position are you in from the beginning? Follow the dynamics carefully and watch for the 'snappy' rhythms. The finger pattern is the same all the way through.*

Swap parts. Which is easier to play?

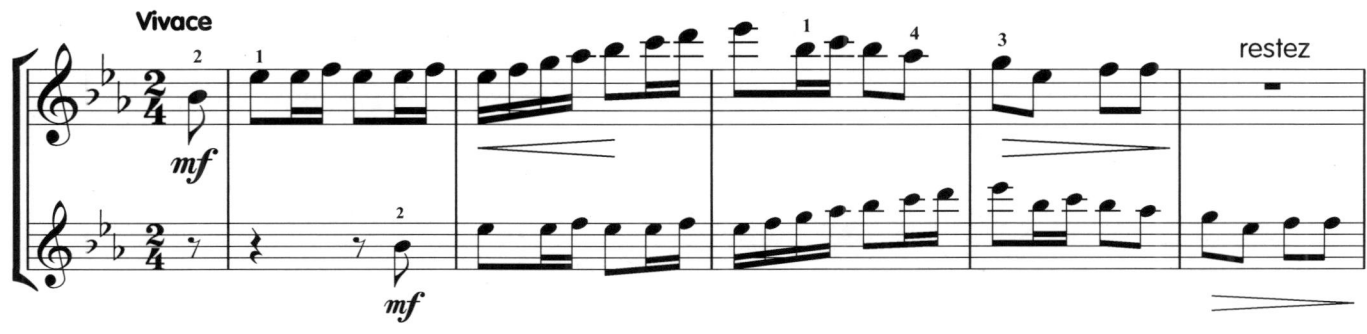

C minor, two octaves

Solos

Follow the **TRaK**

36
- **T** How many beats in the bar?
- **R** Tap through the rhythm of the first four bars with note names (i.e. C Eef F etc.)
- **K** Note the accidentals. C minor has the same key signature as which major?
- **!** Play the scale of C minor before you try this piece.

Play very rhythmically with a firm sound. Try to observe all the dynamic changes.

37
- **T** What is the time signature?
- **R** Clap carefully! Say the note names of the first 2 bars in rhythm.
- **K** What do you notice about the notes of the first 2 bars?
- **?** What position do you start in?

Play through in a spirited manner.   **!** Note all the bars with accidentals.

24

Duets

Follow the **TRaK**

38 *Check the fingering of bars 5 and 6 before you start. Which bars have the 6th and 7th notes of the ascending minor? Remember all the flats and listen to the steady crotchets of the second part as you play through in a dance-like manner.*

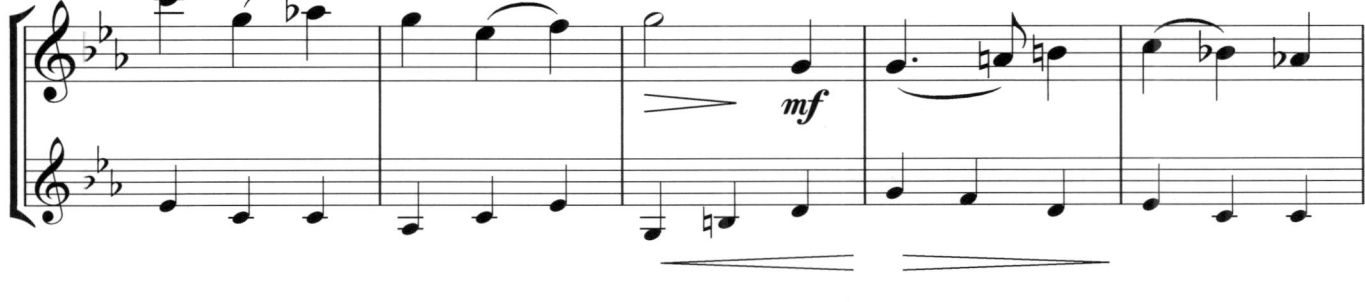

Solos

A♭ major, two octaves

Follow the TRaK

39
- **T** What is the time signature?
- **R** Clap the first two bars with note names (Eef F Eef C Deef etc.).
- **K** What is the key? Which finger pattern should you use in bar 1 and which in bar 9?

A soft spiccato followed by loud accents will help to bring out the playful character of this piece.

? Are there any open strings in this piece? What does **giocoso** mean?

40
- **T** What is the time signature?
- **R** Clap the rhythm of the last 3½ bars before deciding on a speed.
- **K** Name the flats in the key signature. Play the scale of A♭ major.
- **!** Notice how the melody begins on the third beat of the bar. Check where the semitones come and try the first 7 bars all in 3rd position.

Observe the dynamics and articulation. Play through lightly and rhythmically without stopping.

Duets

Follow the **TRaK**

41 *What does **Cantabile** mean? Enjoy this piece.*
Remember 3rd finger D♭s and 4th finger A♭ and E♭.

27

Solos

Follow the **TRaK**

Dominant 7ths

42
- **T** How many beats to the bar and what type are they?
- **R** Name the notes as you tap through the the first 4 bars.
- **K** Find the bars with dominant sevenths or arpeggios in them.
- **?** What do **maestoso**, marcato and **ritardando** mean?

Play through with style. Emphasize the tenuto marks. **?** What type of bow stroke should you use?

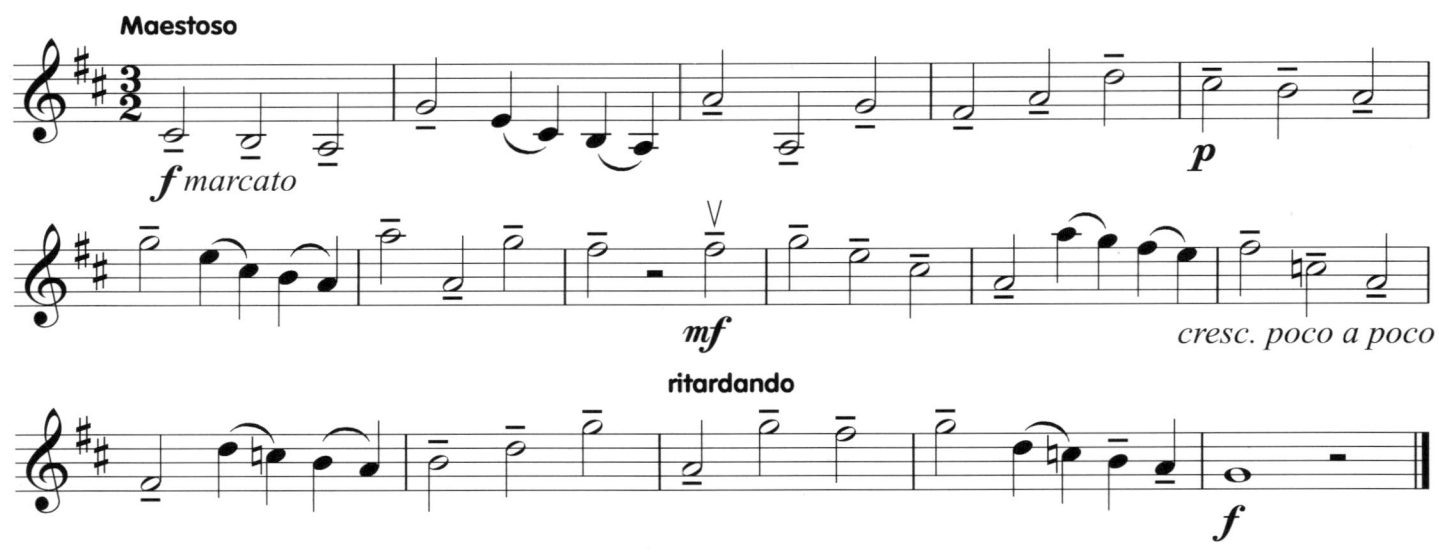

43
- **T** What is the time signature?
- **R** Look at the last 4 bars before deciding on a speed.
- **K** What is the key? Don't be put off by the accidentals!

Keep this spirited and rhythmical, making real contrast in dynamics. **!** Which bars have dominant 7ths and in what key? Name the starting notes.

Duets

Follow the **TRaK**

44 *Check which bars have dominant 7ths. Note that bars 9–12 can be played in either 4th or 3rd position (with a top E harmonic). Always listen for the tune and lessen the dynamic when accompanying.*

Diminished 7ths

Solos

Follow the **TRaK**

45
- **T** What is the time signature and the type of beat?
- **R** Tap notes before you play, feeling 5 beats in a bar.
- **K** How many bars contain the notes of the diminished 7th?
- **!** Play the diminished 7th starting on A, and G minor arpeggio, before trying this piece.

Let this flow. Use all the bow to help the arpeggios sing.

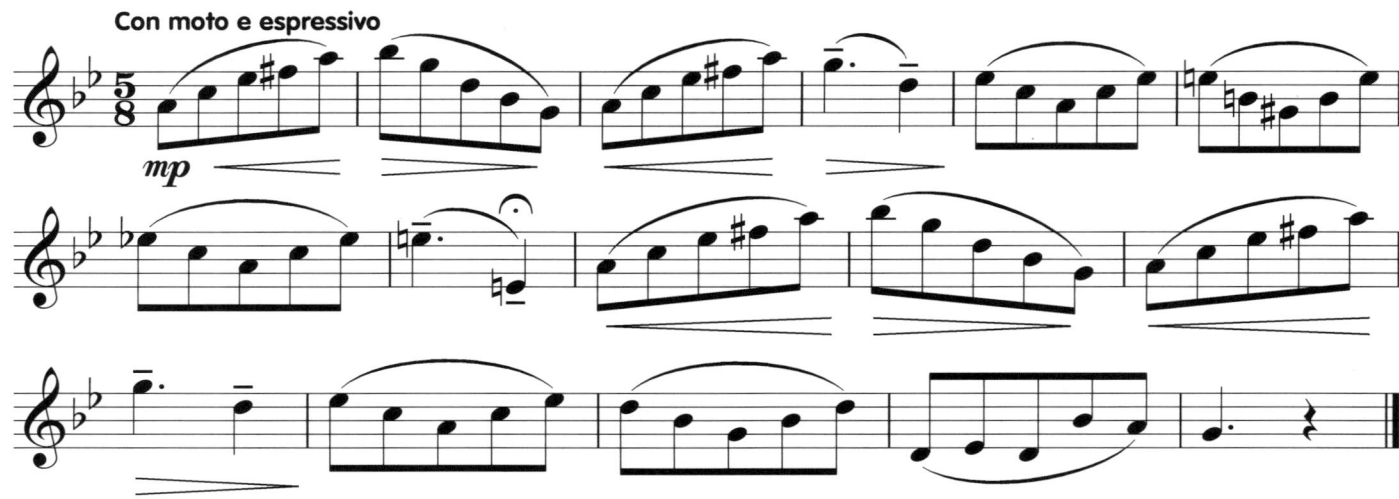

46
- **T** What is the time signature?
- **R** Tap the notes for the first and last 4 bars before playing.
- **K** What is the key?

Remember the accents as you play through with a heavy 2 in the bar.

? How many diminished 7ths can you spot? What does **Pesante** mean?

30

Duets

Follow the TRaK

47 *This duet has a mixture of diminished and dominant 7ths. Can you spot them? Decide on your own fingerings, dynamics and tempo. Give this a title.*

Chromatics

Solos

Follow the **TRaK**

48
- **T** How many beats are there in the bar?
- **R** Tap the notes through slowly and in rhythm, following the fingering carefully.
- **K** Be careful of the accidentals in the chromatic passages.
- **?** What does **Agitato** mean? Play G chromatic scale before trying the piece.

Play this with character and with contrast of dynamic, especially at the end.

49
- **T** How many beats in the bar and what type of beats are they?
- **R** Tap the notes through in rhythm.
- **K** What is the key? Play the one octave chromatic scale starting on open A.
- **?** What does **Lento grazioso** mean?

Play slowly and gracefully, thinking about bow division.

Duets

Follow the **TRaK**

50 *Only play this duet once you have learnt the scale of B♭ in 6ths. Add your own expression marks. What tempo mark would you give the piece?*

Try it with and without slurs for the 6ths. Does this change the mood of the piece?

On your own

Solos

Follow the **TRaK**

Although there are no hints to help you through the following pieces, keep checking the TRaK.